MW01469307

Your Identity

In Christ
Second Edition

Matthew Robert Payne

Your Identity In Christ
Copyright © 2014 by Matthew Robert Payne. All rights reserved.

No part of this publication may be reproduced, stored in a retrieval system or transmitted in any way by any means, electronic, mechanical, photocopy, recording or otherwise without the prior permission of the author except as provided by USA copyright law.

Scripture taken from the New King James Version®. Copyright © 1982 by Thomas Nelson, Inc. Used by permission. All rights reserved.

The opinions expressed by the author are not necessarily those of Publisher.

Published by Revival Waves of Glory Books & Publishing
PO Box 596 | Litchfield, IL 62056 USA
www.revivalwavesofgloryministries.com

Revival Waves of Glory Books & Publishing is committed to excellence in the publishing industry.

Published in the United States of America

eBook: 978-1-312-50581-0
Paperback: 978-1-312-50668-8
Hardcover: 978-1-312-50578-0

To contact Matthew see http://www.matthewrobertpayneministies.net

You can find him active on Facebook in his group "Open Heavens and Intimacy with Jesus"

Copy editing, proof reading, and cover design was done by Freelance workers from Odesk.com

Table of contents

ACKNOWLEDGEMENTS 4
DEDICATIONS 6
INTRODUCTION 8
CHAPTER 1 **YOU ARE PERFECT!** 10
CHAPTER 2 **YOU ARE HOLY AND BLAMELESS!** 16
CHAPTER 3 **YOU ARE POWERFUL!** 20
CHAPTER 4 **YOU ARE HEIRS WITH CHRIST!** 25
CHAPTER 5 **YOU ARE CHOSEN, ROYAL, HOLY AND SPECIAL!** 27
CHAPTER 6 **YOU ARE INHABITANTS OF A BRAND NEW KINGDOM** 30
CHAPTER 7 **YOU ARE RIGHTEOUS, PEACEFUL AND JOYFUL!** 32
CHAPTER 8 **YOU ARE GLORIFIED!** 36
CHAPTER 9 **YOU ARE A CARRIER OF GOD'S GLORY!** 40
CHAPTER 10 **YOU ARE SEATED IN HEAVENLY PLACES WITH CHRIST!** 45
CHAPTER 11 **YOU ARE A SON!** 50
CHAPTER 12 **YOU ARE SINLESS!** 54
CHAPTER 13 **YOU ARE LOVED!** 59
CHAPTER 14 **YOU ARE A CARRIER OF THE KINGDOM!** 63
CHAPTER 15 **YOU ARE PARTNERS WITH GOD IN HIS SUPERNATURAL AND DIVINE NATURE!** 67
CHAPTER 16 **YOU ARE A CITIZEN OF HEAVEN!** 71
CHAPTER 17 **YOU ARE A NEW CREATION! NOT A REMODELLED CREATION.** 73
CHAPTER 18 **YOU ARE CRUCIFIED, BUT ALIVE IN CHRIST!** 76
CHAPTER 19 **YOU ARE A KING AND A PRIEST!** 80

Acknowledgements

First of all, I wish to thank the Trinity for deciding that I would be saved one day. I want to thank the Father for calling me. I want to thank the Holy Spirit for putting the salvation message in a way that I could understand as a child. I want to give very big thanks to Jesus for being my beloved friend though all my years of addictive sin. It is true of me what He said on earth, that one that has been forgiven much loves much.

I want to thank the unknown person who posted all the chapter titles and nearly all the verses that this book contains. I knew when I saw the post that I wanted to read the verses and right away, I decided that I would not only read them but write about them to teach myself these hidden truths. I really got excited as I wrote this, and it is my prayer that as you read, you too, might get excited at what is possible.

I want to thank my copy editor, Melanie Cardano, who carefully went through what I have written and polished it to make me sound better and smarter than I really am. If you need editing done or something to be proofread, you can hire Melanie through Odesk.com, a freelance website.

I wish to thank Maria Quiocho for doing such a wonderful job with the cover. I want to thank Deb for paying Maria through her sowing into my ministry. Maria, a very good artist can be hired for any graphic art though odesk.com

I wish to thank Melinda for loving me and suppoting me so I could pay for the Kindle edition of this book to be made

I want to thank my parents for loving me this far, encouraging and supporting my writing. I hope my mother and father enjoy this latest book of mine.

I want to thank all of you who read this and are ministered to through it. It is my prayer that you meditate on these words until they are a part of you.

I want to thank in advance every person who takes the extra effort and who not only reads this book, but give an honest and frank review of the book on Amazon.

Dedications

Kristen Moore

I want to thank you for being my friend and obeying the Holy Spirit's leading to make me a friend on Skype during our first class together on Inside OutTraining and Equipping School. You know me by the spirit and you treasure our growing friendship. It is my prayer that as we grow together and I have the honor of mentoring you, that you might also follow in my footsteps and become a writer, preacher and prophet to the nations. It is with serious consideration that an author thinks of the people that he knows to include in a dedication page in his book, and I know that I could not pass up the opportunity to bless you by mentioning you.

Harry Limbousis

When I really needed a friend to do a journey with me, God saw fit to bring you into my life. You ae patient, a great listener, a person that wants to understand me and one that encourages me. I am happy to be who I am and delighted to know you and call you my friend. I hope that one day the world will know us as a good duo in ministry. I pray you are as blessed to read this book as I was as I wote it.

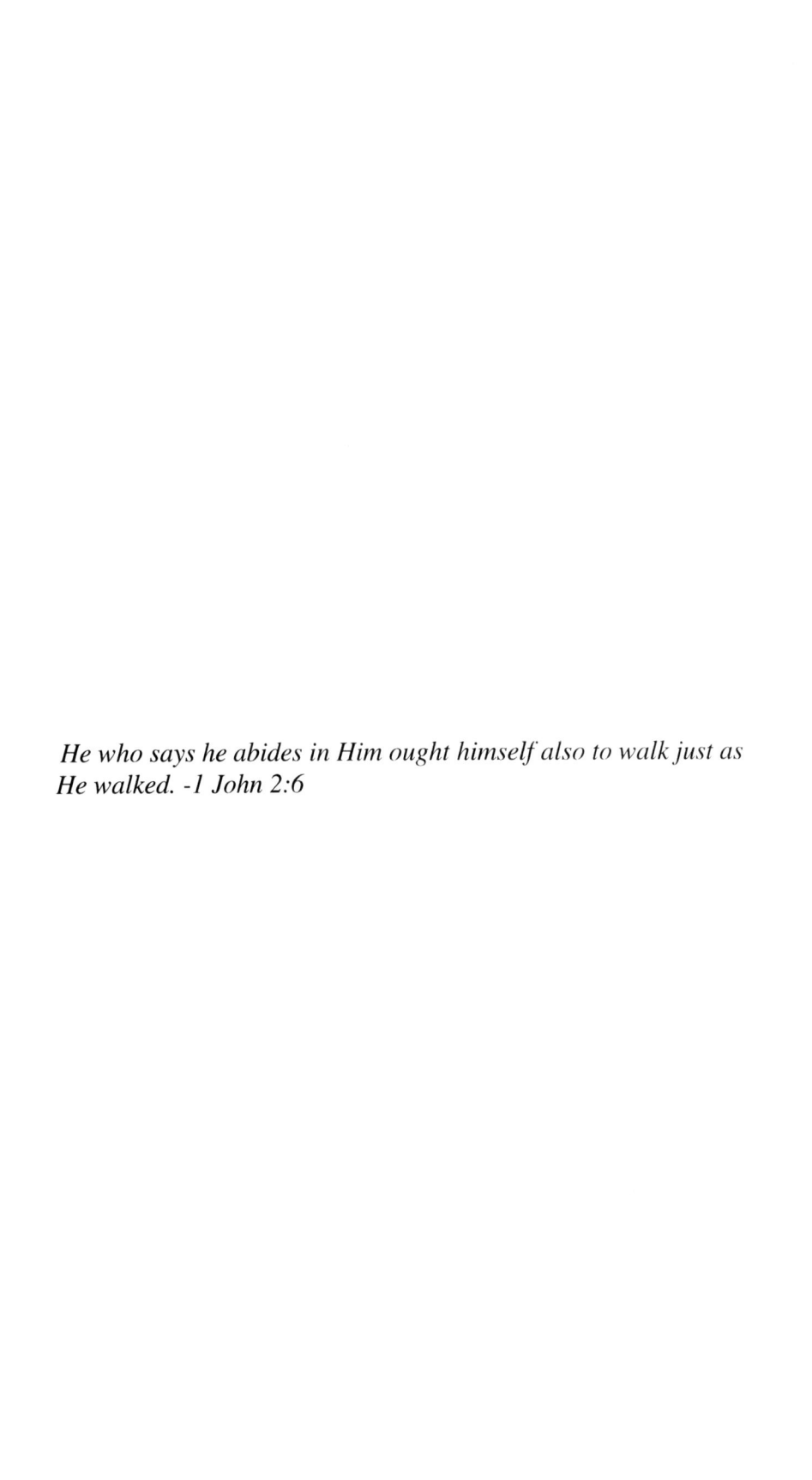

He who says he abides in Him ought himself also to walk just as He walked. -1 John 2:6

Introduction

The Christian life is not an easy life to understand. Life as a Christian in this world should be one continuous journey of discovery and adventure. However, many of us are taught mistruths and seem to settle down to live lives of frustration and complacency. The Christian church sadly operates in a way that allows people to be lazy, not to seek truth, and settle for a lifestyle of man's traditions and religion.

For a number of years, I knew that I will find personal freedom if I could just get a grasp of my true identity in Christ. I heard people speak on the subject and how, when they found out who they truly were, they had started to live a life that was simply outstanding compared to other misinformed Christians.

This book was written as my own act of discovery and I don't think anyone is going to read it as often as I can see myself reading it. I echo the words of Paul when I say that I have not obtained the prize with what I have presented here. I feel it is going to take some time for me to live these truths presented in Scripture in these pages, but no matter what, I press on to the journey set before me.

Years ago in the midst of grave sexual sin I was taken on a vision of Heaven where I met Jesus and was escorted into the throne room by Him to meet His Father. That was one of the best days and experiences of my life. In Heaven Jesus put a New Robe on me. Tt was Joseph's coat of many colors and that was the inspiration for this cover.

Enjoy!

Matthew Robert Payne

March 2014

Update in September 2014

When I wrote this book I was writing it for myself as well as others. I have read this book four times now and more of it is sinking into me. When I wrote it I was struggling with an addiction and since it's first edition was published in March I have been set free of that addiction. We truely do become who we think we are. This is a book that you will need to re-visit more than once. These truths need to go past your head into your heart. It is only when these truths are part of you, that you, like me will begin to act differently.

Chapter 1

You are Perfect!

The idea that we are already perfect may be a foreign subject to you, but that does not mean it is not true. Just as many people who live in this world are unaware of the salvation that is possible through Christ, even people who are living a Christian life are also unaware of that. Through the Holy Spirit dwelling in them, they are already complete and equipped for every good work that God has planned for them.

2 Timothy 3:17

... that the man of God may be complete, thoroughly equipped for every good work.

Many people are unaware that they are made up of spirit, soul and body. When the Holy Spirit comes into a person and starts to reside in our human spirit, the spirit in us is perfect. And from that point on, God sees us as He saw His own Son while He was on earth. Sure, many people might say that the sin they commit each day or week nullifies the assertion that they are perfect. But Scripture says that the son of God and daughter of God has been perfected forever.

Hebrews 10:14

For by one offering, He has perfected forever those who are being sanctified.

When we are born again, when our spirits are renewed by the infilling of the Holy Spirit, we are made perfect and prepared to do the good deeds that God willed for us to do. The same Holy Spirit that rested on Jesus rests on us, and it is only through lack of understanding and knowledge that we think we lack anything to do the will of God in our lives. Think about it, God's Holy Spirit does not come in half, three-quarter and full measure. The Holy Spirit comes down to equip us on how to live God's will.

I have prayed for about four hundred people to receive the gift of prophecy since I have been a prophet myself. These people came to me as they wanted to experience the gift of prophecy and evangelize through the word of God. Everyone I prayed for received this wonderful gift. It makes me wonder if my prayer called up the gift of prophecy in their lives. Or did the process of just coming to me and saying a prayer aroused their faith to realize the gift that was ALREADY in them. I personally believe that every person is equipped to do ministry in the prophetic, for Scripture says that we are created to do good things.

Hebrews 13:21

... make you complete in every good work to do His will, working in you what is well pleasing in His sight, through Jesus Christ, to whom be glory forever and ever. Amen.

There are many people preaching, holding conferences and writing books about how one can be ready for this new anointing and power. Christians move from one conference to another thinking this is what reinforces their divine gift. Sadly, there seems to be a thriving market to endow the believers with everything that they possibly already have.

Colossians 2:8-10

8 Beware lest anyone cheat you through philosophy and empty deceit, according to the tradition of men, according to the basic principles of the world, and not according to Christ. 9 For in Him dwells all the fullness of the Godhead bodily; 10 and you are complete in Him, who is the head of all principality and power.

Many of us think that we need to be like another person. Many of us think that if we could only have Heidi Baker, Rick Joyner or Kris Vallotton pray for us, then we might walk in a more powerful anointing, be able to do more good, and commit sin a whole lot less. However, Scripture says that we are already perfect, complete and faultless from the day we were born again and filled with the Holy Spirit.

Jude 1:24

Now, to Him who is able to keep you from stumbling, and to present you faultless before the presence of His glory with exceeding joy ...

It may be one thing for me to string together a whole lot of verses saying that you are perfect and already complete. And yet, when you lack the power to cast out demons, when you cannot heal people, and when you are still caught in regular sin, the circumstances tend to argue with the assertion that you are perfect and complete.

But does that really hold weight? Just because these conditions are saying that you are not powerful and a sinner, does not mean that Satan weakened you and made unfit for the Kingdom.

There is a place for evangelists to teach people how to share the Gospel with their friends and family. There is a place for effective healers to teach others how to move into healing like them. And there is a place for the Teachers of the Word to teach and equip the saints. It is the duty of the fivefold ministry of Apostles, prophets, evangelists, pastors and teachers to teach the body and prepare them for the works of ministry.

On the subject of the parables of Jesus, I have written a book called *The Parables of Jesus made Simple.* In that book, I teach the reader how to obey the parables of Jesus and live them out in our modern world.

If we speak of prophecy, I have written a book on how to deliver a prophecy and how to find out if you are called to be a prophet. The book entitled, *The Prophetic Supernatural Experience,* has equipped a lot of people to move in the life of the prophetic.

Wisdom can be taught. People can be perfected in life by simply learning that they are already perfect because of Christ.

Colossians 1:28

... Him we preach, warning every man and teaching every man in all wisdom, that we may present every man perfect in Christ Jesus

Some people reading this might say, "No matter how many verses you quote, my experience in my Christian life bears out the fact that I am neither perfect nor complete." Not knowing the truth of who you are could be the very reason you and I are not walking in the path of perfection and completeness.

James says that when we are experienced in being patient, we become perfect, complete and we have everything that we need to do a great job for God in the world.

James 1:4

But let patience have its perfect work, that you may be perfect and complete, lacking nothing

The Christian life can be a bit of a maze. Sometimes, we seem to be running around in circles, lost and wondering which way we should go. I asked an experienced apostle once, a man who would not openly confess that he was an apostle, "Why can't there be a book on how to live the perfect Christian life?" He said that if that book had been written, then the devil would have counterfeited it and the counterfeit would be the bestseller. I was upset, but understood that we all need the Holy Spirit to lead us to the truth.

Being a Christian, as well as embodying Christianity, is not always a walk in the park. For the path could be filled with danger and suffering. Jesus knew his disciples were going to go through these hardships and warned them beforehand. It is through suffering and trials that we learn patience and develop character. We mature and eventually seek peace. The more we understand these Scriptures and truths, the stronger and more effective we become.

1 Peter 5:10

But may the God of all grace, who called us to His eternal glory by Christ Jesus, after you have suffered a while, perfect, establish, strengthen, and settle you.

It is possible to be perfect and complete. If it were not possible, it would mean that the Scriptures we have looked up to would not be in the Bible. When we look at our own life, at our struggles, our sins and our lack of power, we assume that we are not complete. But if you think about it, if the same Holy Spirit that resided in Christ resides in us, then why is it not possible that we can be complete and perfected as well.

2 Corinthians 13:11

Finally, brethren, farewell. Become complete. Be of good comfort, be of one mind, live in peace; and the God of love and peace will be with you.

If you knew Joseph Prince, Joyce Meyer, or Heidi Baker personally, and you show them this chapter and asked them if it is correct, that we can really be complete and perfect, you might be pleasantly surprised.

There is one entity in the world who does not want you to know these things and there are many people in the world who might preach something different, especially if they are selling a book to you. But wouldn't it be cool to meditate on these verses, accept them and start to move into the place where we live in the truth and not with the error that Satan would have us believe? I am the first person to admit that I am not walking in this truth and, like I said in the introduction, I am writing this book to process these truths myself.

Colossians 4:12

Epaphras, who is one of you, a bondservant of Christ, greets you, always laboring fervently for you in prayers, that you may stand perfect and complete in all the will of God.

Chapter 2
You are Holy and Blameless!

If you started in the first chapter, we heard that we are already perfect and complete. Many people, despite the Scriptures shown, would be shaking their heads. It is not because it is not possible, it is not because it is not right; the reason we shake our heads is that for some reason, I have not heard it preached very often. The idea that we do not have to buy that book, or to attend that conference, and the thought that we do not have to have that person, who has a great and powerful anointing, lay hands on us seems foreign to us.

In my own life, no one prayed for me to receive the gift of prophecy. It just started to happen with me. No one anointed me to be a prophet and no mentor coached me into the office of prophet. I struggled, learned, listened to Jesus and the Holy Spirit and finally matured and was promoted by God into the office. No church appointed me, taught me, or ordained me. I was called, trained, equipped and ordained by Jesus Christ, the Anointed One.

This same Spirit that anointed Jesus is effective in making us holy. The Holy Spirit does a great work in us when we accept Jesus Christ as our personal savior. Once again, your mind may argue with the idea, your reasoning and the storehouse of your experience and past teachings may scream blue murder, but Scripture declares that you are now holy.

Colossians 1:21-23

21 And you, who once were alienated and enemies in your mind by wicked works, yet now He has reconciled 22 in the body of His flesh through death, to present you holy, and blameless, and above reproach in His sight— 23 if indeed you continue in the faith, grounded and steadfast, and are not moved away from the hope of the gospel which you heard, which was preached to every creature under Heaven, of which I, Paul, became a minister.

I am not sure about you, but as I write this, my own mind is screaming, "but what about that sin you did last week?" My own mind, that un-renewed mind that does not accept the truth of the Scriptures, wants to say to me that this is a pile of garbage.

My mind, screaming that I am not holy, is the same as the butterfly's mind screaming and saying that he is not a butterfly but still a caterpillar. But Scripture declares as we share in Jesus' death and resurrection that we have become a New Creation. As a New Creation, our old sinful nature has been crucified with Christ and we have arisen as holy.

Colossians 3:12

12 Therefore, as the elect of God, holy and beloved, put on tender mercies, kindness, humility, meekness, long suffering;

Many people are saved through the grace of Christ and are far from kind, humble, meek and long suffering. Many people in the Christian faith seem to lack many of the fruit of the Spirit, so how can we call them holy? The fact is that, whilst we can miss it, when it comes to refined character, the Holy Spirit that inhabits our spirits is missing nothing.

As Christians, we are called to be holy and be set apart. As a Christian, we should no longer be taken in by the lusts of the world. As a New Creation, we should develop in the fruit of the Spirit. We should start to obey the teachings of Jesus and choose willingly to live in love towards God and our fellow man. When we are perfected in love, when all our moves and actions in life are motivated by love, then we we act out what is ours at our new birth: holiness.

1 Peter 1:15-16

But as He who called you is holy, you also be holy in all your conduct, **16** *because it is written, "Be holy, for I am holy."*

Would Peter tell his followers and us readers of his epistles to be holy if it was not possible? Would God in the Old Testament that Peter quotes above, ask His people to be holy if it were not possible? Once again, our mind wants to argue. Our actions, our life in sin, and our former teachings, scream out at us and say that being holy in this world is just not possible. But I do not think that Peter would ask us to be holy if he himself was not holy.

If we cannot be made whole and achieve holiness in this world by the enabling of the Holy Spirit, why would God want us to be so? Many people are happier not knowing the truth. They know that they are sinful and live a life of failure. But at the same time, they cannot accept that there is any way out of it. We live lives of quiet desperation, wearing faces of suffering and wondering like Paul did, who can deliver us from this body of sin.

Before the earth was created, God desired that He might have holy people set apart in love for Him and for others.

Ephesians 1:4

4 *just as He chose us in Him before the foundation of the world, that we should be holy and without blame before Him in love*

Is it too hard to accept that the Holy Spirit gives us the power to walk in perfection? It says in Scripture that every person has the choice to sin or not to sin. We all are given a way out of our sin, a way of escape. We all have the encouragement of Paul to pursue holiness.

Hebrews 12:14

Pursue peace with all people, and holiness, without which no one will see the Lord.

If both Peter and Paul compelled us to be holy, and they knew what they were talking about, then do you think that we might have missed this message? And the fact that not only is it possible, but we can make it a discipline in our Christian life?

Many people will use this Scripture above to beat Christians over the head and warn them that they are not going to enter Heaven without living in a state of holiness. This Scripture, if you have heard it, might not be one of your favorite ones and might bring you into a state of fear for your eternal salvation. That is not why the Scripture was written. It was given to encourage us to pursue holiness and to tell us that it is possible to be holy.

As a believer, we host the very presence of God. As one who is saved, we have the Holy Spirit living in us and therefore we are His temple. God says that the temple in our spirit is holy, so why don't we all act that way?

1 Corinthians 3:17

If anyone defiles the temple of God, God will destroy him. For the temple of God is holy, which temple you are.

Chapter 3
You are Powerful!

About twenty years ago, I walked into a New Age bookshop and went over to the books on witchcraft and started to pick up books on spells and basic witchcraft. I was looking to buy a beginners guide to the subject of witchcraft. As I was pondering my purchase, Jesus spoke to me and told me to leave the bookshop.

I said, "I am only looking to learn about this so that I can bear witness to witches."

I lied to Jesus.

Jesus replied. "You are not trying to buy a book on the subject of witchcraft to bear witness to witches. You are looking to buy the books so that you can learn to practice witchcraft. You are being impatient with Me. You want to walk in power and you are sick of waiting for Me. Leave this bookshop and wait for Me. This is dangerous for you."

I had been a Christian for about twenty years at that point and I wanted to move in power. If you are an average Christian, you might not be looking for books on witchcraft, but you also might want to walk in the power of the early apostles.

Part of the reason that you and I do not walk in power is not because that power is not available to us right now. But, once again, it is because we have no knowledge that it is. Once again, we are going to look at something that is our birthright as a believer, but something we might not be walking into.

Romans 8:11

11 But if the Spirit of Him who raised Jesus from the dead dwells in you, He who raised Christ from the dead will also give life to your mortal bodies through His Spirit who dwells in you.

Did you catch that? The same Spirit that raised Jesus from the grave dwells in you and I. That is some power is it not? The world, men and false teachings would have you and I believe that power only goes to the leaders and ministers of the Gospel. The whole church is divided over the power of the Holy Spirit.

Some churches believe that the gifts of the Holy Spirit and therefore the power of the Holy Spirit ceased from operating in the church after the last of the apostles died. They have their reasons for this and, because of this belief, these churches do not often see a demonstration of the power of God.

Some churches believe in the gifts of the Holy Spirit, but many of these church attendees believe that the power only gets given to the leaders and ministers of the Gospel. The average Pentecostal or charismatic Christian believes in miracles, healing, signs and wonders, but doubts that they can be the one who does these things.

Paul says that the same power that raised Jesus from the dead resides in us! That sure sounds like good theology, but it does not sound right to us. Once again, the enemy does not want us to catch onto this truth. Would it be possible, therefore, for one of us ordinary people to cast out demons and heal those who are sick? If the average reader, or the average person who is saved, caught on to the truth contained in this verse, the whole world would be turned on its head.

Here is a testimony of an ordinary person who does ministry in a counselling situation:

A man in his 30's with 5 children came for counselling and his background scared me. Drugs, alcohol, food addiction, raised by a violent father, clinical depression, unemployment, new age witchcraft and poverty. Worst of all, he came out of Mormonism. He had been talking to demons since he was a grade schooler. I know the Joseph Smith demons. Very smart and violent.

After I explained what was wrong with him, what kind of spirits he had and how they were destroying him, we went to prayer. Fortunately, he was humble and open minded. As I was leading him through prayers of God's love and mercy, it started. He began to weep profusely and shake all over.

He was infected with a Legion of spirits and they all started to resist. A desperate move with the Holy Ghost in the house. I was dreading the Moroni spirits. Suddenly, he started coughing and heaving as the first layers of monsters began to come out. It went on for half an hour and then the Mormon demons manifested. Hate, rage, murder, death. He began to scream so loud I had to plug my ears. It went on for 30 minutes. When the spirits were all gone, he received his Gift of Tongues and was gloriously healed. He was literally speechless and could hardly believe it. I gave him his homework and some hugs. Mk. 1.

Ephesians 3:20

Now to Him who is able to do exceedingly abundantly above all that we ask or think, according to the power that works in us

Did you catch that Scripture? Now, to God, who can do exceedingly, and abundantly above all we can ask or even dream up. We have a power that is in us, that not only can do what that man did in the above testimony, but that can do great things that are more than we can even think of. Many people would love to walk in power. Many people would love to be able to heal the sick. Many people would love to be able to prophesy. This Scripture says that God in us can cause us, through His power, to outdo all of our dreams and thoughts put together.

So what is stopping us? The simple knowledge that all things are possible to those of us who believe. Do you believe that you can do the impossible? Do you believe in that verse that says God can work in us to such an extent that He can exceed our greatest thoughts and dreams of ministry? I do not know if you are getting fired up by this book, but I know that writing it is making me feel very good.

My testimony:

One day, a friend of mine came and sought me out at my church. He did not attend my church each week, but came with the express purpose of seeking me out. When church finished, he approached me and asked if we could go out to get something to eat.

As we walked to Burger King in the city of Sydney, Australia, he told me that his back was in severe pain and that the pain killers he was on are not helping him. He told me he was on the maximum dose of pain killers and still he was in severe pain each day. He said, "I wish God could heal my back."

I put my arm around him and hugged him. I said, "You know I would heal you if I had the faith."

He nodded and said, "Yes, I know Matthew."

About twenty minutes later, at Burger King, Jesus told me to lay hands on my brother as He was going to use me to heal him. I asked my brother if I could lay hands on him and pray. He said yes and I prayed for God to heal his back.

My friend has been free of that back pain for ten years now. You see, twenty minutes beforehand, I had said I would heal him if I had the faith and yet when Jesus said for me to pray for him, my faith had not changed. I simply did something exceedingly, and abundantly more than I could ever imagine.

Wouldn't it be cool if we not only professed to be Christians, but also walked in Christ's power through the Holy Spirit? Wouldn't it be good to not only be known by our love, but to be known as the person to go to when you need a miracle? Paul might not have had the best speech and way of preaching, but he came with the power of the Holy Spirit. So can we!

1 Corinthians 2:4-5

4 And my speech and my preaching were not with persuasive words of human wisdom, but in demonstration of the Spirit and of power, 5 that your faith should not be in the wisdom of men but in the power of God.

Mallory on Facebook read this chapter and commented:

I remember saying that I wanted more of Jesus. I wanted to be able to see life extended to others because I could walk in His presence successfully. I wanted to see others set free to live the abundant life that Jesus offers to everyone. Then, as words of the prophetic came faith did arise and I first began to launch out in the intercessory ministry, and soon I was hearing words of the prophetic for other people. I was lead to some online ministries that train and equip for service. I feel that I am now walking in the thoroughly equipped phrase of my life.

Chapter 4

You are Heirs with Christ!

How would life be like if you were born a prince, the son of a King? Would you live your life differently, dress differently and behave differently? Many people look at the princes and princesses in the world and silently wish that they were one of them, and yet we all are sons and daughters of a King and joint heirs with Jesus Christ!

Romans 8:15-18

15 For you did not receive the spirit of bondage again to fear, but you received the Spirit of adoption by whom we cry out, "Abba, Father." 16 The Spirit Himself bears witness with our spirit that we are children of God, 17 and if children, then heirs—heirs of God and joint heirs with Christ, if indeed we suffer with Him, that we may also be glorified together. 18 For I consider that the sufferings of this present time are not worthy to be compared with the glory which shall be revealed in us.

The people who grasp this promise and truth of Scripture, live a far different life on earth than the rest of us. They do not live without hardship or suffering, because that was promised to all of us who chose to follow Jesus. But the people who know they are heirs with Jesus, live a lot more prosperous and successful Christian life.

Do you know God as your daddy? Do you know Him in a deep and loving way or are you living a long way from Him, and hoping that He does not get angry with you? Do you know God as a loving God, one who wants to treat you as a son or a daughter? Does His love get lavished on you? Do you draw close to Him so that He would draw close to you?

James 4:8

8 Draw near to God and He will draw near to you.

Many of us stay well clear of God as we think He is angry and wants to punish us for our sins. Many of us live under the Old Covenant and do not see God as a God like Jesus. People who do not know they are loved lavishly by God, miss out on the blessings that come with a deep and personal relationship with God. People who fear God will not draw close to God, but stay away in some sort of holy fear.

We need to know that we are just as important to God as His Son was to Him. We need to know that we share in the inheritance of Jesus. Now, Satan is quite happy for us to never know this. Just like a prince who wanders off from His mother and father as a young child when they are visiting India and can be found living as a beggar on the streets, so too are we who do not know that we are heirs with Jesus Christ.

What would you do if Jesus appeared to you and gave you a Visa card and a PIN number to an account that had no limit to the money? Most of us would learn very fast how to spend money and our lifestyle would drastically improve. Well, as far fetched as it seems, Jesus has already done that with his deposit of the Holy Spirit in us. We just have to believe it and walk in it!

Chapter 5

You are Chosen, Royal, Holy and Special!

I am not sure about you, but it fills me with such delight to know that before time began I was chosen and predestined to become a son of God. I am so pleased that I am saved, jumping for joy as I write this, to lay hold of the truth that God chose me before the very foundation of the world.

Ephesians 1:4

4 just as He chose us in Him before the foundation of the world, that we should be holy and without blame before Him in love

God not only CHOSE us, but like we have already discussed, He made a way and gave us the power to become holy and without blame in this world. We live in a world gone wrong and every person is looking for answers. And as the world gets darker and darker, we are in a position to be without blame and to be the ones who give them the answers pertaining to life.

Does it excite you that you were chosen? I have to admit that it makes me sad that some people have not been shown the Kingdom of God and therefore have not yet been chosen. But the joy that fills my heart to know that my loving Father chose me before he created the world in which we live on is amazing.

It is not only the verse above that says that I am chosen Here is another one:

1 Peter 2:9

9 But you are a chosen generation, a royal priesthood, a holy nation, His own special people, that you may proclaim the praises of Him who called you out of darkness into His marvelous light

This verse is full of wonder. You are part of a chosen generation. I believe you were put on earth to witness the last great outpouring upon the world before Christ returns. We have been chosen by God to birth a new revival and harvest of souls just before Jesus returns. I am so happy that God chose me. I am so happy to be a good friend of His Son.

This verse also says that we are royalty and we are priests. We heard in the last chapter that we are co-heirs with Christ. We are royalty, so we need to become aware and start to act and live like we are sons and daughters of a King. We would be doing a lot better in this world if we all walked and talked as if we were really royalty. We would hold ourselves better and we all would be in a better condition if we knew our rights.

In the Old Testament, priests made the sacrifice for the people. Today, we can help people come to Jesus as well as administer grace through our love and forgiveness of others. Today, we can serve God, if we can only believe and walk in it by healing people and casting out demons.

The church can and will in the future become a holy nation. We, as a group of believers, can learn to be in the world, but be different and more outstanding than the world. We, as a group of believers, can be that safe place of refuge where the hurting and the desperate can run to. I am sure that the apostle Peter knew that the church could become a chosen and holy priesthood to the world.

This verse says that we are special and it is so exciting to be called special. Don't you want to get that into your spirit man? You are special and set apart. You are a treasure to God. Though you are flesh, you are made of good stuff. God delights in us. Have you ever been told that God and Peter think you are special? I mean, if we are special, this means we can do things that are different from the other people who are part of this world.

Colossians 3:12-13

12 Therefore, as the elect of God, holy and beloved, put on tender mercies, kindness, humility, meekness, long suffering; 13 bearing with one another, and forgiving one another, if anyone has a complaint against another; even as Christ forgave you, so you also must do.

We are the chosen and elect of God. We are the special people who have been set aside to light up this world and drive back the darkness. We can achieve this by being loving, holy and full of Godly character. We are called to be tender, merciful, kind, humble, meek, and patient with people. The world is used to people wanting their own way and being selfish. And yet, as the Holy Spirit resides in us and as we abide in the vine which is Christ, we can change the world one person at a time by the way we live and act.

We can act holy and righteous and do the right thing. When a person is hard to cope with, we can bear with that person, forgive that person and lead them into the right way of living. When people sin against us, we have the power to forgive the people just as Christ forgave us. We can be radical lovers. Not only can we know Jesus or know the Father, but the Holy Spirit can manifest through us in such a way that as priests, we can draw all men to Christ and His love.

If you can believe it and receive it, you are chosen, royal, holy and special.

Chapter 6
You are inhabitants of a brand New Kingdom

Many people, even after they are saved, that is, born again, still continue to live by the rules of the Kingdom of this world. They are unaware that they are in a New Kingdom, that the rules have changed and they do not have to perform the same way anymore.

Colossians 1:13-14

13 He has delivered us from the power of darkness and conveyed us into the kingdom of the Son of His love, 14 in whom we have redemption through His blood, the forgiveness of sins.

Instead of being a sinner, they are now a saint and a citizen of Heaven.

Instead of being filthy, they are washed clean as wool, as white as snow and are righteous and holy.

Instead of being alone, they are the elect and chosen of God.

Instead of being worthless according to their job or education, they are special, chosen and holy.

The new Kingdom has a new way of operating. There is little need to strive to be loved. You are loved without measure. You are the beloved of God and you are a righteous son or daughter. You are a precious son or daughter of God and no more do you have to perform to be holy and set apart. It is what Christ did that set you apart and made you special.

Instead of having to come to God with special duties and sacrifices, you can rest in the fact that Christ, who is sinless and perfect, laid down His life and made a sacrifice for you that was forever accepted in your place.

Instead of having no power or ability to fight the wrong things that we are tempted with each day, we are given the Holy Spirit to enable us to walk in perfection and holiness. Where once we were bound and held by sin and bondages, Christ's power came to break every chain and set the captives free.

The enemy would like for you to be unaware of this new reality. He would prefer you to think that while you sin, you are a sinner. He does not want you to know you are now in the Kingdom of Light and that you now have a new nature that does not need to fall into sin. As long as you are convinced that you are a sinner and not a righteous saint, you will remain in a sinful lifestyle.

Many people teach that a person who has been born again into the Kingdom of the Son can lose their salvation by sin and therefore go to hell. There are quite a number of very popular preachers who say a person can be born into the Kingdom of the Son and then fall away and go back into the Kingdom of darkness. This is a sad teaching and helps put fear into people. This fear, rather than releasing them into righteous living, keeps them bound in a sinful lifestyle.

If you go around saying you are a sinner, you will continue to sin. If you go around saying that you are righteous and holy, soon enough, your body and mind will be transformed and begin to line up with the new confession.

Chapter 7
You are Righteous, Peaceful and Joyful!

Many people would equate their pastor or priest as righteous but do not see themselves as particularly righteous. Many people assume that because they have sinned in their life, they are not righteous. They assume that only people who do not commit any wrong can be righteous. With that in mind, many Christians live quiet lives of desperation, wondering what is different in them, why they were not saved from sin.

2 Corinthians 5:21

21 For He made Him who knew no sin to be sin for us, that we might become the righteousness of God in Him.

The truth is that we have been made righteous through the death and resurrection of Jesus Christ. God made Jesus sin, so that we might have a divine exchange and wear His robe of righteousness now on us.

Once again, preachers and Satan would have us believe that if we are sinning, then we are not righteous. People are left so confused, but here it is said as plain as day, that Jesus became sin so that we might be made righteous.

What is the point of the enabling of the Holy Spirit, if one cannot defeat sin? The way to defeat sin is not to strive against it, but positionally see yourself as righteous and live from that mindset. When you understand that you are perfect, complete, holy, chosen, set apart and righteous, you begin to get it into your mind that it is possible to be a New Creation and walk like it.

Years ago, no man had run the mile in under four minutes. It was understood to be impossible for a man to do. One day, Roger Banister ran a mile in under four minutes. What the world of runners thought was impossible suddenly became possible. Since then, hundreds of people have run the mile in under four minutes. People only needed to believe that it was possible. People need to know it is possible to live a life free of sin.

What if I said to you that I have met two men who confessed to me that they rarely sinned? When I asked them if they sinned, I was shocked to find that it was a very rare occurrence for them. Rather than making me depressed, it made me excited. I knew if they could do it, then it was possible for me to do it in my life as well.

We discussed that Paul and Peter urged people to be holy. We agreed that Paul and Peter would not be asking people to do something that they were not already doing. Don't you see? When you know you are seen as righteous by God, it is easier to conform into that image.

We are not meant to go through our lives living in shame, guilt and condemnation. We are instead meant to live in joy and peace through the manifest presence of Jesus resting in our lives.

Romans 14:17

For the kingdom of God is not eating and drinking, but righteousness and peace and joy in the Holy Spirit.

Many people are crippled with guilt and shame. As a person who was addicted to pornography for 34 years, I lived in a constant cycle of shame, guilt and condemnation. Every few days, I would fall again and I would run away from God and His presence for a day or two. It was not until I learned that I was forgiven and loved despite my sin that I reached the stage where I could walk in the Spirit and overcome the addiction.

People should know us for the joy that is within us. People should see us as happy and joyful. People should know that the Christian life has real rewards and is a life of peace in the midst of the same storms that batter the lives of people who are not saved. People who are not saved should look at us and see something that they want. They should not see us as the angry, upset, religious and judgmental people that many of them see.

It is possible to walk in the knowledge that you are loved, accepted and righteous even in the midst of sinning. I needed to get to a point where I knew I was loved no matter what I was doing, to finally reach a point where I could allow God to give me the grace to overcome my addictions. Being set free was a miracle, but it was a miracle that was birthed in the knowledge and understanding that I was considered a righteous son BEFORE I was actually set free.

Jesus told a parable about a feast. At the feast, people were given wedding clothes and they were seated. At these feasts, each of the guests were given a robe that was the same, so that every person, no matter what their wealth or social standing, were dressed the same. At this wedding feast, a man was found who did not have the wedding clothes on. He would have been given the clothes, but had decided not to put them on and dress like the other people. The host of the feast had him kicked out of the feast. This man is someone who has been given the robes of righteousness of Christ and yet has decided to live in his own self righteous acts and deeds. Jesus wants you to accept that you are seen by Him as righteous and He wants you to work that out in your life until you have overcome and really are living a life free of sin.

There are preachers who preach all about the Ten Commandments and all about the Law of God, and say that you have to stop doing certain things to be righteous. But who can ever get motivated not to do something by being told you cannot do it? People who preach the Law, instead of teaching you how to walk in love and righteousness, actually strengthen the hold of sin in your life.

You are free to be righteous, joyful and peaceful. Do you want to be?

Chapter 8

You are Glorified!

I did not fully understand what the word glorified meant, and seeing as I was going to write about it, I had to go to an online dictionary. This is what it had to say about glorified:

*glo·ri·fy [**glawr**-uh-fahy, **glohr**-]*

verb (used with object), **glo·ri·fied, glo·ri·fy·ing.**
1. To cause to be or treat as being more splendid, excellent, etc., than would normally be considered.
2. To honor with praise, admiration, or worship; extol.

We are to live such a life on earth as we mix with others so that we bring praise, honor, worship and admiration to the name of Jesus. As we go about our life as a Christian, the name and the person of Jesus should be glorified.

Jesus also promises that if we bring Him glory, He will allow us to be glorified in the eyes of the people of the world. Rather than being despised and looked down upon with scorn and derision, Jesus promises that those who abide in Him will be honored and admired by the world.

I guess if you are a person who says you hate gays, hate people who do abortions, and you are constantly judging people without offering love and answers, you might be a person who is looked down upon.

Jesus wants to raise people as followers after Him; loving, powerful, and who have the answers to life's struggles on this earth. These are people who are full of unconditional love and power to transform lives, people that other people can honor and respect.

John 17:10-22

10 And all Mine are Yours, and Yours are Mine, and I am glorified in them. 11 Now, I am no longer in the world, but these are in the world, and I come to You. Holy Father, keep through Your name those whom You have given Me, that they may be one as We are. 12 While I was with them in the world, I kept them in Your name. Those whom You gave Me I have kept; [c] and none of them is lost except the son of perdition, that the Scripture might be fulfilled. 13 But now I come to You, and these things I speak in the world, that they may have My joy fulfilled in themselves. 14 I have given them Your word; and the world has hated them because they are not of the world, just as I am not of the world. 15 I do not pray that You should take them out of the world, but that You should keep them from the evil one. 16 They are not of the world, just as I am not of the world. 17 Sanctify them by Your truth. Your word is truth. 18 As You sent Me into the world, I also have sent them into the world. 19 And for their sakes, I sanctify Myself, that they also may be sanctified by the truth.

20 "I do not pray for these alone, but also for those who will [d] believe in Me through their word; 21 that they all may be one, as You, Father, are in Me, and I in You; that they also may be one in Us, that the world may believe that You sent Me. 22 And the glory which You gave Me, I have given them, that they may be one just as We are one:

One of the reasons why the Christian world is scorned and overlooked in the West is that they preach a whole lot of rules and regulations, but they fail to demonstrate the answers to life's problems. Many Christians in the West are broke, sick and full of worry. Other people, when they see a Christian in our world is just as worse off as they are, deny the Christian faith and assume that the faith being preached by the average church is no longer relevant to them.

Jesus was not talking about a church like that in these passages. He was praying for the disciples who lived by faith, who went from town to town casting out demons and healing the sick among them. These disciples had given up their life of wealth and prosperity and have learned to abide in Jesus Christ and His ways,.To the point where they were really effective and where everything they did prospered. Jesus wants His people to prosper and to be an answer to the world and its struggles. People who live by faith, and live in their Christ-won identity will be honored and respected by the world.

Many people have got a natural aversion to suffering with Christ. Paul did not have that mindset, where he showed that he wanted to develop fellowship in the sufferings of Christ. Jesus admonished us to deny ourselves and take up our cross and follow Him. In denying ourselves and doing the things God calls us to do, we may suffer like Jesus and the apostles did, and yet at the same time, have our names glorified.

Romans 8:17-18

17 and if children, then heirs—heirs of God and joint heirs with Christ, if indeed we suffer with Him, that we may also be glorified together. 18 For I consider that the sufferings of this present time are not worthy to be compared with the glory which shall be revealed in us.

There is one way to live a Christian life: in ignorance or disobedience. And then there is another way to live with full understanding of who we are in Christ, and the power and anointing in our lives that flows from that.

Every Christian, no matter which way they are currently living, whether they are informed of their rights and power, or whether they are ignorant like I have been for many years, are chosen and predestined by God. Each of us who have been saved, have been called to be of service to the Lord, and each of us is considered guiltless and holy by the Lord of Hosts. Each of us was called and encouraged to prosper in the Christian life and to shine as a bright example to the world.

Romans 8:30

30 Moreover whom He predestined, these He also called; whom He called, these He also justified; and whom He justified, these He also glorified.

It is only lack of knowledge and discernment of who we are that keeps us bound and ineffective in this world. The knowledge known to a person who prophesies to and heals people can be known by us. The people who have a ministry that has plenty of financial support, who move in signs in wonders and change cities that they attend to, know things that we don't know. But we can know these things, and knowing our rights as a Child of God through Christ can help us to move to a place where we will not only bring glory to Jesus' name but our own lives will be honored and glorified by the people of the world.

I commend you to abide in Jesus and His commands and pray with Jesus that your knowledge and wisdom in the things of God might increase. So that the people of the world and other Christians will recognize you like they did Peter, that surely you have been with the Lord Jesus.

Chapter 9

You are a carrier of God's glory!

You would expect that God alone would possess glory. It is funny to consider that the glory of the Lord can rest on us. You'll remember when Jesus was transfigured on the mountain and His face and clothes shone like the sun. Many people would consider that would not be possible, but a promise in the Old Testament speaks prophetically about our faces shining.

Isaiah 60:1-3

60 Arise, shine; For your light has come! And the glory of the Lord is risen upon you.
2 For behold, the darkness shall cover the earth, And deep darkness the people; But the Lord will arise over you, And His glory will be seen upon you.
3 The Gentiles shall come to your light, And kings to the brightness of your rising.

This passage speaks of the unbelievers (i.e. Gentiles) being attracted to the brightness and light on your face. This passage says that great darkness will cover the earth when this passage of prophecy is due to be fulfilled. I guess you can accept that the world is getting pretty dark now. So is it possible for the glory of the Lord to rise upon us, to such an extent that our faces shine like the sun? It sounds weird, right?

My Testimony

One day about twenty years ago in the city of Brisbane, I was walking through the city streets and I noticed every person in the street staring at me. Some would be walking along and they would stop when they see me, their mouths would drop open and they would just stare at me.

Some of them would come up to me and ask me if I had a light for their smoke. Some would come and ask me if I had a spare smoke. Some would ask me if I had the time. This was before there were cell phones with time on them, and I was not wearing a watch so it seemed strange that they would come and ask for the time. I quickly worked out that these people approaching me were seeing something and so I tried to be loving and courteous to all of them.

I went to a public toilet to look at my face and check if I could see what the people were staring at, but I could not see it. The people looked at me all day and later in the day, I come to realize what they were seeing. It was about 7:30 pm at night and I was seated listening to a busker play some contemporary songs that I liked. A youth started to ask me some questions.

He asked, "What do you believe in?"

"I am a Christian, I believe in Jesus," I replied and then turned back to the busker.

"I am a Christian as well. But what is different about you?" he continued.

"I am Spirit filled." I said.

"I am baptized in the Holy Spirit as well," he said, "but what is it about you?"

Getting frustrated with this youth distracting me from the music, I turned, exasperated, and asked him, "What is it about me? What do you think is different about me?"

"Your whole face is glowing. Have you seen anyone put a torch into their mouth and made it shine through the skin and the whole face lights up? Well, you are just like that. Your whole face is

shining. How do you make your face shine like that?"

I was shocked and I really did not have an answer to give him. I was tired and run down and though I was an obedient Christian, in some respects, I still walked in a sinful lifestyle. I was amazed that he was saying that my face shone.

Another time, I was in a shopping center when I noticed a whole lot of people turning and staring at me. I knew that I was shining again. This time, I made sure that I was loving and courteous to the people that I met and interacted with as I knew what they were seeing and I wanted to be a good example.

I approached a food shop where there were about fifteen people in line waiting, some being served, but about ten people waiting to be served. As soon as I got to the back of the line, one of the service ladies saw me and asked me right away what I wanted to buy. All the people waiting in line before me, turned to look at me and I was sure they could see my shining face. I said, "No, I am okay to wait. You have all these people waiting in front of me for service."

Some of the waiting people smiled at this. Some of them were confused why I refused service, maybe thinking that I was deserving because I was not an ordinary person. I was happy to wait until all the people before me were served before I allowed them to serve me. On that day, I felt I was a good witness for Jesus.

Another time, I saw about a hundred angels turn up. Jesus told me it was Valentine's day and the visit was His way of loving me on our special day. I was with a friend and as we left the eatery, the angels came with us. My friend started to tell me that a whole lot of people were looking at me. On this occasion, I knew I was shining with the glory of the Lord again and I knew that the hundred angels had somehow brought that glory to my face.

I am not the only one that this can happen to. Scripture says:

2 Corinthians 3:18

18 But we all, with unveiled face, beholding as in a mirror the glory of the Lord, are being transformed into the same image from glory to glory, just as by the Spirit of the Lord.

It is possible that you are already shining with a measure of the glory of the Lord in your life. Some of the signs that your face is shining a little with the glory of the Lord are these:

- People who are begging in the street will approach you and ask you for spare change. People who beg, try and ascertain good natured people that they believe will give to them. They do not ask everyone, but only people that they think are kind and with a giving nature. If you always go out with friends, but no one approaches your friends and the beggars only ask you for spare change, this is a sign that they see glory on your face.

- People approach you often in the streets and ask you for directions. You may be walking towards a person or a couple and see people walking past them and not see them asking anyone for directions. When you get to them, they ask you if you could give them directions. These people can see a glory on your face and they read it as a person who would be helpful to them and help them if they can.

- Another sign of glory on you is when people begin to open up to you and tell you things that they have never told anyone else. People just seem to always cry on your shoulder and feel that you can be trusted.

The glory of the Lord is available to all of us. Seeing the glory on a person is like seeing the glow on a mother who is expecting. The glory of the Lord is attractive to people. If people approach you to ask you for spare change all the time, God knows you can afford it, so give to them.

I hope this has been helpful.

Mallory on Facebook read this chapter and commented:

I have had many people tell me recently that they see super grace and anointing on me. People do share their problems and issues with me. However, many times I see a name and I'm lead to go into intercession for them. The revelation that others see the glory of God on me is very precious. Some people have asked me to pray about joining their ministry team, that is new but encouraging.

Chapter 10

You are seated in Heavenly places with Christ!

Everybody needs a champion. Everyone needs an example to live by and to emulate. As Christians, we are encouraged to live like Jesus. He did not just come to save us from our sins and pay the price for sin. Jesus also came to give us a model of what it looks like to live by following the Spirit.

Every day Jesus walked in the Spirit, every day He saw visions and interacted with Heaven. Jesus was a forerunner for us, He lived and performed under what some people call an "open Heaven." Jesus often said He only did what He saw His Father doing. Are we to assume that Jesus was making up this statement? Or did Jesus, like prophets of old, have visions of Heaven and His Father before He ascended to sit at the right hand of Him?

Ephesians 1:20-23

20 Which He worked in Christ when He raised Him from the dead and seated Him at His right hand in the Heavenly places, 21 far above all principality and power and might and dominion, and every name that is named, not only in this age but also in that which is to come.

22 And He put all things under His feet, and gave Him to be head over all things to the church, 23 which is His body, the fullness of Him who fills all in all.

Could we, as His body, walk in the fullness of Jesus? Are we called to live like Jesus? Have we got the same access to Heaven as Jesus? Are we really citizens of Heaven? Are we already seated in

Heavenly places?

Ephesians 2:4-10

4 But God, who is rich in mercy, because of His great love with which He loved us, 5 even when we were dead in trespasses, made us alive together with Christ (by grace you have been saved), 6 and raised us up together, and made us sit together in the Heavenly places in Christ Jesus, 7 that in the ages to come, He might show the exceeding riches of His grace in His kindness toward us in Christ Jesus. 8 For by grace you have been saved through faith, and that not of yourselves; it is the gift of God, 9 not of works, lest anyone should boast. 10 For we are His workmanship, created in Christ Jesus for good works, which God prepared beforehand that we should walk in them.

What does it mean that we are seated with Christ Jesus in Heavenly places? Does it mean that we can spiritually open our eyes and see Heaven? Is it really our right as a Christian to actually visit Heaven? Is it true? Can the average Christian go to Heaven and meet Jesus, angels and saints?

Yes, they can. Yes, being seated with Christ actually means that this is our right. We can travel to Heaven by being in the body (in our minds) or out of the body (with our spirits leaving our body) and see and interact with all that we see there. The only thing that stops the average, normal Christian from going to Heaven is knowing that they can go, and having the faith to go. There is a school on Facebook called *"Inside Out Training and Equipping School"* that will teach you your rights when it comes to going to Heaven and then equip you to have a vision of Heaven via Skype and report back to the other students on what you saw.

My testimony

I had been to Heaven many times and one night, as I was lying on my bed speaking to Jesus, I appeared in Heaven in my mind. I was still lying on my bed, but in my mind's inner screen where you see memories, I could see Heaven. I was seated in a deck chair and Jesus was seated on another and he passed me a drink called a Pina Colada (It is made of rum and pineapple juice.) We drank and chatted on the back deck of my house in Heaven over looking water. This was the first visit to what I would discover was a mansion in Heaven. I was amazed that I could taste the pineapple in my mouth on earth.

The second time I went inside my house in Heaven, I saw my cat that had died when I was eight years of age. The cat prophesied to me, which a few weeks later came true. In the house, I saw aquariums built into the walls of the house. Out past the deck on the ground floor was a pool and in the pool was tropical fish. When you swam in the pool, you could touch the fish. A pipe ran from the pool to the house and all through the walls of the house, there were aquariums where fish followed you as you walked from room to room. On that visit, the cat prophesied to me, and a fish called Harry spoke to me. A few weeks later, I made a new friend on earth who had the name Harry.

The third time I saw my house in Heaven, I saw my lounge room. There was a painting on the wall of a lion with children in the background. When you approached the painting, the lion and children came alive. And when you walked through the painting, it was a portal to where children play in a park in Heaven. The park is a special place in Heaven that I like to visit when I go there where children that were aborted play. On that same day, I saw a painting of the woman who washed Jesus' feet with her tears and who wiped His feet with her hair and then put perfume on them. When you approach that painting, it comes to life and when you go through that painting, it is a portal to Mary Magdalene's house in Heaven.

Over the course of nine visits to my house, I saw that I had two pools at my house. One is outside, past the deck and one is an inside pool on the second floor. There is also a coffee shop that seats fifty people, a movie theatre that seats a hundred people, an office, and a personal library on the second floor. Downstairs is a commercial kitchen and I know it has a third floor that I have not seen yet. I know I have more to see on the first floor, the whole third floor to see, and I am not sure if I have seen all of the second floor yet.

This is your right. This is your inheritance. If you have not been to Heaven as you read this, join Inside Out on Facebook and write to me and tell me when you have!

So many people assume that they can only go to Heaven when they die. So many people think that only people who write books get the chance to go to Heaven while they are alive. People wrongly assume that only special people get to go to Heaven. I will tell you this. Because Jesus shed His blood to save you, you are already special.

Have you ever met a person who comes under a lot of attack, but just keeps on going? Have you met those people who just seem to endure one trial to the next and who do not complain, but just seem to get nicer and more and more full of grace and love? These are people that Jesus calls overcomers. You do not become an overcomer when you die. You are an overcomer as you overcome trial after trial. Jesus promised this to all of us.

Revelation 3:21

21 To him who overcomes, I will grant to sit with Me on My throne, as I also overcame and sat down with My Father on His throne.

My Testimony

On my first visit to Heaven, Jesus took me into the throne room. When I got to the front, God asked me to come and sit on Jesus' throne right on His right hand side. God spoke to me, Jesus sang to me and I met many of the saints of Heaven. After the event, I was tripping out a bit about me sitting on Jesus' throne and Jesus led me to this verse in Revelation.

One of the rights we have as sons and daughters is to visit Heaven and even have Heaven visit us on earth.

Chapter 11

You are a son!

We spoke in the last chapter about an overcomer not being someone that you become when you die, but as someone that you are right now as you go through trials in life and cope with them. Living victoriously as a Christian in a modern world makes us an overcomer and this is what Jesus had to say about it the book of Revelation.

Revelation 21:7

He who overcomes shall inherit all things, and I will be his God and he shall be My son.

It is something that is hard for me to get my head around, to be a son of God. I guess that I have walked in so much sin in my life that I never felt worthy to be a son of God. But I have gone through many trials and have obeyed Jesus in many things and I know prophetically, I am an overcomer, as I have heard God say it often about me.

It is awesome to be considered a co-heir with Jesus. To inherit all things, like a son of a rich father on earth lives to see his inheritance, so are we. It is so overcoming and edifying to contemplate as I write. You may see my writings infused with wisdom, but honestly, I chose to write this little e-book to reinforce these concepts to me. It is such an overwhelming thought to be considered a son. It is so rich, so profound and powerful, if we could just get hold of it.

2 Corinthians 6:18

"I will be a Father to you,
And you shall be My sons and daughters,
Says the Lord Almighty."

My Testimony

I grew up with a really angry father. I feared my father and it seems that our house was made in such a way that we had to walk on egg shells, hoping not to do something to make our father explode.

About twelve years ago, a prophetic friend of mine started to cry. He looked at me with tears in his eyes. I asked him what was wrong. He told me that God had a message for me. I asked him what the message was.

He said, "God says that he is not an angry God. He is not like your father. He wants you to draw near to Him and come to get to know Him. He is not angry with you and will not get angry with you when you mess up."

I was wrecked. I was in tears and in the past 12 years, I have taken baby steps getting closer and closer to my Heavenly Abba.

Romans 8:15-17

15 For you did not receive the spirit of bondage again to fear, but you received the Spirit of adoption by whom we cry out, "Abba, Father." 16 The Spirit Himself bears witness with our spirit that we are children of God, 17 and if children, then heirs - heirs of God and joint heirs with Christ, if indeed we suffer with Him, that we may also be glorified together.

The Abba is a really affectionate way of addressing a father. It is like a child running to a father's arms after he has been away for a week on business saying, "Daddy, Daddy." It is deeply personal and affectionate. Most people seem to have my experience with God as a distant and angry God who will throw a thunderbolt at you if you mess up.

Sadly, many people see a God taught by preachers based on an image they get from the Old Testament. They do not seem to have the same image of Jesus and yet Jesus said that if you had seen Him, you had seen the Father. Paul taught that Jesus was the exact image of the Father. We have those verses in the Bible, but still, we fear God and walk with distance between us.

We all need to get to a place of proper teaching and healing so that we can run into the lap of God in Heaven and call Him Abba, Daddy, Papa God. We need to be close and very intimate with Him. This is our right as a Child of God. We should live free of fear and not settle until we are in that place.

Before time began, God knew He was going to save you. Before the earth was created, He knew you were going to read this and have a yearning in your heart to know your identity. Before you were born, you were predestined to be adopted into the family of God.

Ephesians 1:5-6

5 Having predestined us to adoption as sons by Jesus Christ to Himself, according to the good pleasure of His will, 6 to the praise of the glory of His grace, by which He made us accepted in the Beloved.

It is just so amazing that before we were born, we were chosen to be saved. It is such a wonderful joy to know Jesus and to know that He wanted me and you. It is such an honor to be counted as one of His Beloved.

I heard it taught once about adoption in Jesus' day. Apparently, any man with means could adopt a son or daughter in those times. It was a custom in those times that a father could sell a child into slavery up to three times in the child's life and then pay money to redeem them back. A father who fell on hard times could actually sell his son and when better times came, he could go and buy his son back. He could do this three times as I have said, but anyone who adopted a son could not sell the adopted son into slavery. This is so precious, because it means when the Father bought us with the blood of Jesus off Satan, we cannot go back into slavery to sin. The adopted sons in that day were protected from being sold. This gives a new meaning to being adopted sons. Jesus, the natural son, was given as a sacrifice and died for our sins, but we have more rights as adopted children.

By having faith in Jesus, we are made sons as this verse clearly says:

Galatians 3:26

For you are all sons of God through faith in Christ Jesus.

I know that I need to meditate on this more. If I really knew my identity in Christ, I would be a lot more powerful person in the Kingdom of God. Yippee, I am a son!

Bonnie Foster read this chapter on Facebook and commented:

I struggled with the idea of God being my Father. I didn't grow up with a Father so it was hard for me to know exactly how a father is supposed to be. I have come to know God as my Father and I am a daughter of a King and that makes me a royal priest. I am loved by my Father, I am protected by my Father and I have my Father's DNA. I am loved in the Beloved. Matthew has brought this reality to me and showed me my need to come to my Father more boldly. So many in the body of Christ do not know who they are in Christ so they live beat up and defeated lives. If only they knew how much God truly loved them and who they are in Christ then they would know that we are more than conquerors and are victorious in Him.

Chapter 12

You are sinless!

When we do not know our rights when it comes to the law, then injustices can be done to us by the police. When we do not know our rights as a tenant, then injustices can be done to us by landlords and other tenants. So, too, with us and our rights and identity as a Christian. When we do not know our inheritances as a child of God, we live in a manner that is lacking.

I am not sure about you, but I have met two Christian ministers who had little to no sin in their life. One of them said to me that he had conquered sin and no longer willingly sins, and the other one said that he does not sin very often. To people who have never heard anything like that before, they would have an issue with these verses as it would not seem to make sense to them.

1 John 3:9

9 Whoever has been born of God does not sin, for His seed remains in him; and he cannot sin, because he has been born of God.

1 John 5:18

18 We know that whoever is born of God does not sin; but he who has been born of God keeps himself, and the wicked one does not touch him.

I really liked the apostle John and yet I could never really reconcile these verses with my life. To me, living a life free of sin was impossible. My understanding was that we were all sinners saved by grace. My understanding was that we all sinned and each time we did, if we repented, things were fine. I had no idea that you could possibly live a life free of sin.

I had one of the aforementioned ministers living at my house for a month and about 3 weeks into the month, I was so impressed with this holy man's behavior that I asked him outright,

"Do you sin?"

"No Matthew, I don't." he replied.

"Is that possible?" I asked.

"Yes, it is."

"Where is that said in the Bible?"

"Romans chapter 6 addresses it at length as well as other places."

Well, that was interesting. I was totally shocked. He told me about being a New Creation and how our sin nature was nailed to the cross and we came out of baptism with a new nature that did not have to sin. Now, many people are not walking in this holiness, but I know my friend was not lying to me on that day and it makes a lot of sense. Read it for yourself. We do not have to sin anymore as a child of the King.

Romans 6:1-7

6 What shall we say then? Shall we continue in sin that grace may abound? 2 Certainly not! How shall we, who died to sin, live any longer in it? 3 Or do you not know that as many of us as were baptized into Christ Jesus were baptized into His death? 4 Therefore we were buried with Him through baptism into death, that just as Christ was raised from the dead by the glory of the Father, even so we also should walk in newness of life.

5 For if we have been united together in the likeness of His death, certainly we also shall be in the likeness of His resurrection, 6 knowing this, that our old man was crucified with Him, that the body of sin might be done away with, that we should no longer be slaves of sin. 7 For he who has died has been freed from sin.

Of course, this is in the Bible, but it is not often taught. And who has been fortunate enough to meet and know two apostles personally and had the courage to ask them if they sin personally? Satan has a vested interest in keeping the church blissfully unaware of the realities of the New Creation. Whenever we think sin still has a hold on us, then we are bound by that false reality. When we know for sure that we are a New Creation and that we do not have to sin like John says above in the verses I quoted from 1 John, then we can and will walk free of sin.

God has given us the power of the Holy Spirit and He has given us the grace in that power to walk free of sin. It is our inheritance as a child of God. And yet when you do not know it, you live like a poor beggar who does not know his real father is a king.

1 John 1:7-9

7 But if we walk in the light as He is in the light, we have fellowship with one another, and the blood of Jesus Christ, His Son, cleanses us from all sin.

8 If we say that we have no sin, we deceive ourselves, and the truth is not in us. 9 If we confess our sins, He is faithful and just to forgive us our sins and to cleanse us from all unrighteousness.

The above verses mean, if you say you have never sinned, then you are a liar. But if you are now walking free of sin, then you are simply walking in the Holy Spirit. I am not sure if you have ever noticed it, but these verses say that Jesus is faithful and just to forgive our sins and cleanse us from ALL unrighteousness. That is not just the sins you did last week he will cleanse you from, and you continue to sin. No, that means that He will give you a cleansing that will allow you to walk in holiness, free of all unrighteousness.

Read on:

Romans 6:17-22

17 But God be thanked that though you were slaves of sin, yet you obeyed from the heart that form of doctrine to which you were delivered. 18 And having been set free from sin, you became slaves of righteousness. 19 I speak in human terms because of the weakness of your flesh. For just as you presented your members as slaves of uncleanness, and of lawlessness leading to more lawlessness, so now present your members as slaves of righteousness for holiness.

20 For when you were slaves of sin, you were free in regard to righteousness. 21 What fruit did you have then in the things of which you are now ashamed? For the end of those things is death. 22 But now having been set free from sin, and having become slaves of God, you have your fruit to holiness, and the end, everlasting life.

Can you see it? We are free. We have been set free. We simply have to walk in it and live in it.

Now you might have read this chapter and, like me, it really has not sunk in yet and it may take some time. It is hard to accept that you can walk without sin. Many of you might be just looking forward to the next chapter and dismissing this chapter. Many of you might be thinking that when I said I knew of men not walking in sin, that I had been lied to. I am not sure what all of you are thinking, but it is possible to walk without sin. John wanted people to know that and he said it clearly in the verses that we mentioned. But for you and I who are still coming into this reality and trying to reconcile that we are a New Creation that does not need to sin, let this closing verse encourage you.

1 John 2:1-2

My little children, these things I write to you, so that you may not sin. And if anyone sins, we have an Advocate with the Father, Jesus Christ the righteous. 2 And He Himself is the propitiation for our sins, and not for ours only, but also for the whole world.

Chapter 13

You are loved!

So much personal spiritual power comes to a person when they are convinced once and for all that God loves them. For me, I was friends with Jesus for most of my life, and yet my relationship with God was distant at best. As I have mentioned, I grew up with an angry father, and I superimposed this father figure on God. For most of my life, I assumed that God was an angry God, ready to swat me like a fly if I stepped out of line. And though you do not know much of my story so far, many of my years as a Christian was involved in grave sexual sin.

When you have a lifestyle of sin, it is hard to maintain a great relationship with God. For many years, I did not know what true repentance was and did not know how to do it, so I was bound in chains to my sin. However, through those years, Jesus was my friend. Though I did not attend church for many years, I could feel Him there, just one conversation away, always ready to comfort me. Many of us know because God sent His Son Jesus to earth to die for our sins, that he loved us. All of you will know this verse.

John 3:16

16 For God so loved the world that He gave His only begotten Son, that whoever believes in Him should not perish but have everlasting life.

What a tremendous demonstration of God's love for us that he would send His only Son to live on this earth, show us the way to live, and then to die a horrific death on the cross. What a tremendous demonstration of faith that was by Jesus to die that death, drinking the cup of suffering that His Father had for Him to do. Sometimes I reflect on the death that Jesus went through and it brings me to tears each time. Yet, few of us reflect on the pain that it would have caused the Father to watch His Son be crucified. Many of us know the story of Abraham being asked to sacrifice his son, yet I am not sure many of us could have been that obedient with our son. God, through His enormous love for us, had His son slaughtered for us and our liberation. Not so that we might perish, but for us to live in communion with Him both on earth and eventually in Heaven.

On the night just before he was arrested, he said a prayer for us and His disciples as recorded in John chapter 17. Part of that prayer says:

John 17:23

23 I in them, and You in Me; that they may be made perfect in one, and that the world may know that You have sent Me, and have loved them as You have loved Me.

Jesus shares in this prayer that we, as His followers, are loved just as the Father loved Him. Did you hear that? We are loved as much as Jesus is loved by His Father. That is amazing for me to hear as I contemplate this verse and write about it. Do the people in your world know that God loves you as He loves Jesus? I am just so overcome with the knowledge that God loves me as He loves Jesus.

It may be fun for you reading this. You might be a lot more confident of God's love for you than I am. I was prompted by the Holy Spirit to write this book, mostly because God wanted me to meditate on these verses and process them by writing about them. I am sure that this book will help many people, but I know it is helping me to write it.

I have had hundreds of prophecies in my life by equipping people to speak in prophecy and having them prophesy over me for practice. Hundreds of times God has said that He loves me and is proud of me through prophecy. Even whilst I was bound in sin, God was saying that He was proud of me and that He loved me. There is so much liberty found in the knowledge that God loves us.

Do you know that God loves you just as much as He loves His perfect Son, Jesus? Can you capture that? Does it resonate with your spirit? Can your spirit handle knowing that you are loved beyond measure, or are you stuck in sin and doubting God's love for you like I was? You might be thinking that all you need to do is get your life together and cure your sin to be loved and accepted fully by God. God says differently. He loves you right now and will be with you as you give your life to Him and let his power and grace heal and lift you.

We are the children of God now. We have been born again and accepted into His family.

1 John 3:1

3 Behold what manner of love the Father has bestowed on us, that we should be called children of God! Therefore, the world does not know us, because it did not know Him.

I am sure that sin is why so many people do not come to God. So many people live a life far away from God and their lifestyles of sin keeps them from approaching Him. Yet, as a child of God, our sins should not keep us from our loving Father. He holds our answer. He is the One who can heal our pain and our hurt. We should not hide from Him. We, like the prodigal son, should come home and let our Father heal us and fix us up.

You might live a pretty righteous life. You may be already living a very successful Christian life and not relate well to this writing about being stuck in sin. Perhaps, you might want to know that even Jesus goes from deeper to deeper intimacy with His Father each day. In Heaven, there is no one who has arrived. All of them are going from glory to glory. Each day in the presence of the

Lord, the saints of Heaven learn more, grow more, and move to a greater glory. So, even if you live a life with little to no sin in it, a more complete revelation of God's love for you will always take you further and deeper into a fruitful relationship with God.

Stephen read this chapter on Facebook and commented:

The great approach of God and his magnificent love for us is not only found in Jesus' life, death and resurrection, but also in Jesus' glorious arrival and birth. That is something we can consider every Christmas! When we were separated, lost from the Father; sinners and companions with death, Jesus died for us only after he was in God's great love first sent to us. Jesus lived, breathed; powerfully ministered on earth to all, he was witnessed by all who followed him and believed in his name. The Bible says that no greater love has anyone but that love which was laid down, crucified and put to death for his friends. This is the love Jesus displayed; a selfless, unconditional, perfectly undeniable and tremendous love for you and for me. Whether sinner or saint, good or bad, there are no criteria because this law covers all and embraces all. That same love shifts even the most vile into a glorious eternity of everlasting love!

Mallory read this chapter of Facebook and commented:

I remember a time when I was a young believer, while I was praying and worshipping I went deep in the Spirit. Shortly, after a time I was flooded with the Love of the Father. It went on and on. Wave upon wave, intense feeling of love, I could hardly catch my breath. It would intensify and intensify I really thought I would die. I broke it off. I had to stop the connection or I would collapse. I am very sorry that I did not pursue it. It was my first and last experience like that. I'm believing for something more.

Chapter 14

You are a carrier of the Kingdom!

One of the biggest lies propagated by the enemy through our personal thoughts or by teaching is that some people have the Kingdom of God operating in their life, and others like us do not. Yet, Jesus had this to say to the people in His day.

Luke 17:21

21 Nor will they say, 'See here!' or 'See there!' For indeed, the kingdom of God is within you."

It is quite disheartening sometimes to hear of great ministries and to watch them. I am not sure about you, but I want to serve the Lord as much as I possibly can. I look at people who have been used powerfully in healing and who have international ministries and I get sad that it is not me. Is that true of you as well?

When I do that, I am seeing that person who has the kingdom of God works through them in a powerful way and I do not. Yet, Jesus says, "I have not said, 'See here and, see there!'" I am to come to the knowledge that the kingdom is in me and it can be as great a measure in me as I have the faith for.

I have been reading books by Roger Sapp, who is a preacher and healer. He has been used in the last 17 years to heal about 30,000 people. He is an exceptional writer and I have tremendous joy reading his books. He personally did not have much success with healing people, healing only about two people a year. Until he spent 2 years meditating Jesus' miracles in the Bible to build His faith that Jesus is Our Healer today just as much as he is our Savior. After a lot of meditating and prayer, Roger took off and started to see a lot of success in his ability to heal people.

I have had people prophesy over my life and tell me I am going to be used powerfully in healing, and for years I have been searching for training. Well, Roger has a book on all the healing ministry of Jesus and the apostles in Acts, and he has a 120 page book study companion with 1200 questions about the book. The book is called, *Performing Miracles and Healing,* for those of you who are interested.

I feel if I take the time to read this book and answer all the questions and learn to meditate on the 104 meditation cards on healing that he has made, that at least, I will be better equipped to pray for the sick when I encounter them. I know that I have to overcome my doubts about healing and grow in faith that people can be healed today, and that is the Father's will of people. I know if I invest time in it, it will not be wasted. I hope some of you might embark on this journey with me.

So much is not accomplished in this world for God because we do not know our personal identity in Jesus. To consider that the Kingdom of God is within us, just like it was in Jesus, is something that is amazing for me. I feel that we need to know that God wants to use us for more than just sitting in a church pew and paying tithes. God has a world that needs to be saved, impacted, loved and healed. God wants to use us. Are you up to being used?

I have the gift of prophecy and, when led by the Lord, I can tell people all about themselves and talk about their future. Many thousands of times, I was led by the Holy Spirit and have approached people in the streets of my city and shared a personal message of God with them. I am very experienced with this gift, and I still find it amazing every time I speak to a person and see their feedback. I am just so amazed every time God allows me to get it right. I do not often get it wrong. Here is an encounter I had yesterday and what I posted on Facebook.

PRAISE REPORT

I was accosted by a person trying to raise funds for a charity. The young girl had a nice tattoo saying "Keep true to what you know" or something like that and I made a comment about it and a comment, a word of knowledge about one of her character traits.

I told her that sometimes I spend about $150 every two weeks on self publishing books so I cannot give to her charity and she said that was cool. I told her another thing about her character, another word of knowledge. She asked me how I knew things about her.

I told her I was a prophet. I said I am like a clairvoyant, only mine is a gift from Jesus. She asked me to tell her more about her and her future. I continued with three more words of knowledge about her, how she was a free spirit, and she has not committed to any religion yet as she was still doing research.

She was gobsmacked with what Jesus was telling me about her. We got onto the subject of the Bible and she asks why would a 2000 year old book be relevant today. So I started to quote verses about sins that are mentioned in there and asked her if those sins are still relevant.

We talked about evil and how it really exists. She came back to the Bible and said how do we know it was not just made up by some men 2000 years ago. I told her that I know a book that proves the Bible was written by inspiration of God, and how God had sealed the word.

I asked her if she had a pen. She got her pen out and I wrote down the name of the book. I told her that if she adds me as a friend on Facebook, I will even buy it for her. She promised she would read it.

What an awesome encounter

P.S. The book is called The Seal of God by a man with the last name, Payne, like me.

I have written a book about prophecy and the life of a prophet called *The Prophetic Supernatural Experience* and through people buying it each month, I am slowly equipping people to walk in prophecy and understand the life of a prophet. I know personally that just as God uses the Holy Spirit in me and my faith in prophecy, He can soon use me in healing the sick when I study.

Do you want to be used? One way to be used is to come into the knowledge that the same Holy Spirit that worked in Jesus is in us. One way to be used is to know that God wants to use us and He is willing to train and equip us to be used. To be effective, though, we need to know who we are in Christ Jesus.

Chapter 15
You are partners with God in His supernatural and divine nature!

We learned in chapter 12 that we have a new nature and not the old sinful nature that we were born with. We need to get a good hold of this fact, so Satan does not dupe and convince us that we are the same old sinners that we always were. We have been baptized into a new nature and with that nature, we can live without sin in our life. It may be hard to consider, and I was getting a lot of attacks today about what I wrote in chapter 12. Satan does not want us to know that it is possible to live a righteous and holy life, but it is so possible because we have a new divine nature.

2 Peter 1:4

4 By which have been given to us exceedingly great and precious promises, that through these you may be partakers of the divine nature, having escaped the corruption that is in the world through lust.

This verse maintains that we have escaped the corruption of the world. You might not have escaped yet, but this verse promises that you can! We can live a pure and holy life through this divine nature and the empowering of the Holy Spirit.

Like me, you might not be totally free of wrong thoughts and actions each week. You might not like the way someone speaks to you and wish they would just shut up. You might not have had the patience to spend time with that needy person who wanted to speak to you and you excused yourself. Each week, there may be examples of how you did not walk like Jesus would have if He were you. Scripture declares, though, that we should be walking like Jesus. Once again, the challenging verse comes from John, the disciple Jesus loved.

1 John 2:6

6 He who says he abides in Him ought himself also to walk just as He walked.

This is a big call. John is saying here that if we are in a right relationship with Jesus, that we should be just like He was to the world. Can you imagine that? Can you imagine being just like Jesus to the world?

I have sat in churches for many years and never heard people preach on these verses out of 1 John that were used in chapter 12 and here. The verses of 1 John just seem to be too hard for people to come to grips with. I guess that many pastors have not reached the state in life where they are walking sinless so they are unable to preach on a verse that calls us to live in that way. If that is not the reason, I cannot understand why they have not preached on these verses.

To walk like Jesus on this earth, is that really possible? Is it really true that we can be like Jesus in all we say and do?

Jesus, in the commandments that He taught us to walk in, showed us how to walk in love. Jesus shared with us in the Gospels how we are to treat each other. Walking like this, obeying Jesus, through the empowerment of the Holy Spirit, is how we express this divine nature in us. John had this to say about Jesus' commandments.

1 John 2:4

4 He who says, "I know Him," and does not keep His commandments, is a liar, and the truth is not in him.

John does not mince his words here. He says it quite clearly that the people who can really claim to know Jesus walk in His ways. There are many people sitting in the pews each week who are not coming under the Lordship of Jesus. Many people say He is their Savior, but Jesus is not their Lord and someone who they obey each week.

Sin is defined as *"missing the mark."* It is an archery term that describes a person missing the bullseye on a target. The bullseye in the Christian life is simply the commands of Jesus Christ. When we do not live by them, which is live in love towards God and our fellow man, we sin.

We have been given the gift of the Holy Spirit. We have been given the instructions on how to live. We are partakers in the divine nature. We should be able to live in a better way.

Many people fear the coming troubles that are going to manifest in the world. Many people have a real fear of these storms that are going to come and test every person in the world. Obeying Jesus and doing what He taught us will also help us in those days. Jesus had this to say about his commands and people who put them into practice.

Matthew 7:24-27

24 "Therefore whoever hears these sayings of Mine, and does them, I will liken him to a wise man who built his house on the rock: 25 and the rain descended, the floods came, and the winds blew and beat on that house; and it did not fall, for it was founded on the rock.

26 "But everyone who hears these sayings of Mine, and does not do them, will be like a foolish man who built his house on the sand: 27 and the rain descended, the floods came, and the winds blew and beat on that house; and it fell. And great was its fall."

The storms might not have hit yet. The people of the church who do not obey Jesus in their life might not be getting affected yet, but the days are coming where being a person who walks like Jesus does will protect us.

Jesus says the people who love Him, obey His words and commands. And He says the way you tell that people do not love Him, is that they fail to do what he said.

John 14:23-24

23 Jesus answered and said to him, "If anyone loves Me, he will keep My word; and My Father will love him, and We will come to him and make Our home with him. 24 He who does not love Me does not keep My words; and the word which you hear is not Mine, but the Father's, who sent Me.

We have the divine nature. We are a New Creation and we have the Holy Spirit in full measure, so we can do great things. I pray this has been a little convincing to some of you. You might want to do a search of the Commands of Jesus on Google and start to walk in them. After all, what would Jesus do?

Chapter 16

You are a Citizen of Heaven!

When you give your life to Jesus, you become a citizen of Heaven. You are taken from the normal human condition and made into a super human who is able to manifest the glory of Heaven in your mortal body. You are no longer normal. You are invited to a fellowship with God, Jesus, the saints who have passed on, and the angels of Heaven

Philippians 3:20-21

20 For our citizenship is in Heaven, from which we also eagerly wait for the Savior, the Lord Jesus Christ, 21 who will transform our lowly body that it may be conformed to His glorious body, according to the working by which He is able even to subdue all things to Himself.

Of course, one day, we will all have a body that is new for the life in Heaven, but right now, we are accepted in the brethren of Heaven. I wish that more people know their birthright as a child of Heaven. I wish more people knew that they were seated with Christ in Heavenly places.

Ephesians 2:6

6 And raised us up together, and made us sit together in the Heavenly places in Christ Jesus,

One time, I was talking to a Christian friend who was a bit down and depressed. I asked him to hold my hand and told him to imagine what I was describing. I told him he could see a fountain with a lion and a lamb walking around at the base of it. When he could see that, I described children that were behind the fountain and he could see them. Then, I had one of the children come up to him and speak to him and he started to get emotional. I told my friend that he was in Heaven and these children were the children of Heaven. I said that whenever things get too much for him, he should go in his mind to the children and let them comfort him.

I wish that I could do that with all of you who are reading this. One day, I will teach people how to go to Heaven. As I have mentioned, *Inside Out Training and Equipping School* on Facebook can help people go to Heaven and have visions.

It is one thing to talk about God and to know about God, but it is quite another thing entirely to meet with Him and converse with Him in Heaven. It is another thing to have Him come and sup with you in your own house on earth like it promises He will. God is a good God and we are walking like a person with a limp when we do not know our identity in Christ. Jesus wants us all to know who we are and I hope that you are being encouraged by this book.

There are many stories that I could share about going to Heaven, but I would be more encouraged if you could write to me and share your story of your Heavenly encounters.

Chapter 17

You are a New Creation!
Not a remodelled creation.

Let us start with our Scripture:

2 Corinthians 5:17

17 Therefore, if anyone is in Christ, he is a New Creation; old things have passed away; behold, all things have become new.

Now, this is saying if you are walking hand in hand with Jesus, the sinful life that you are into should pass away and ALL things should become new in your life. We are created anew. We are not a remodelled job, but we are completely new. Satan will fight you hard on this one if your experience is anything like mine. Satan will tempt you to sin and if you fall into the sin, he will let you think nothing has changed and that you are NOT a New Creation and indeed all things HAVE NOT become new.

The truth that we have to live in is this verse. We ARE a New Creation and ALL THINGS have become new. Just like Peter walked on the word of Jesus when Jesus said "Come" to him and he walked on water, so too, we are to walk on this verse. It may not seem true to us. We might not "feel" new, we may not be "acting" new; but God's Word, when properly understood, does not lie to us.

Walking in the New Creation reality is powerful. Many people in these days of grace are starting to prove that it is possible. We know the apostle John walked in this or else he would not write that we can walk like Jesus and live a sinless life. John would not commend the church to walk without sin unless he was already doing it.

Are you not excited? Do these eternal truths covered in this book excite you? I know I am getting really excited. It is true, it is true, it is true, we can walk and talk and act just like Jesus in this age. Can you sense my excitement? There is nothing like writing a book to teach yourself. I know there are scholars and people who are a lot more eloquent who could write this book, but I have been chosen to write it and most of it was to teach and encourage me. I write books for people to buy for 99 cents or to get free on free kindle days, I do not write them to make money. When I wrote my book on the parables, I learned a lot about the parables. As I wrote the book on the prophetic, I learned a lot from the experience. When I wrote my biography, I processed a lot and had a lot of healing happen and as I write this, I am just feeling so empowered and excited about who I really am.

I am but a simple guy who understands like Paul that without the cross, I am nothing.

Galatians 6:14-15

14 But God forbid that I should boast except in the cross of our Lord Jesus Christ, by whom the world has been crucified to me, and I to the world. 15 For in Christ Jesus, neither circumcision nor uncircumcision avails anything, but a New Creation.

We do not have to live a life of religion, of what to do and what not to do, to be accepted by God. We can come out from the yoke of religion with its Do's and Don'ts and we can simply start to walk in our status as a New Creation. We can be free of the circumcision.

We can do mighty exploits with the freedom and liberty that the power of the cross brings us. We can live in resurrection power where the old life has passed away and a new life has sprung forth. We can be enabled by the Holy Spirit, we can be called, trained and equipped and minister in the harvest for we know that the need is great and the laborers are few and far between.

Don't you want to be new? Don't you want to walk unencumbered? Well, you are! You just need to see it and walk in it!

Chapter 18

You are crucified, but alive in Christ!

Let us have a look at our text:

Galatians 2:20

20 I have been crucified with Christ; it is no longer I who live, but Christ lives in me; and the life which I now live in the flesh, I live by faith in the Son of God, who loved me and gave Himself for me.

Do you find that is true of you? It is no longer you who live, but Christ who lives in you? It may not be true of you at the moment, but it was true of the Apostle Paul's life. Paul talked about his struggle with sin and then he came to the conclusion that he had to die and live in the New Nature. Paul did not go around the world sinning, preaching, healing the sick, and then sinning again.

I personally doubt that the Apostle John, who has been bold enough to say a number of times during this book that as Christians we should not be sinning, that he was sinning. I feel that Paul and John and all the apostles who knew Jesus, lived holy and righteous lives.

I know, not all of you have personally met an apostle and lived with him for three weeks. I know, not all of you had the courage to ask him if he ever sins. I know that many of you were not here for that conversation that he had with me where he spoke for about half an hour showing me in Scripture why I do not have to sin anymore. I am not sure that even if you heard him, whether you would have held onto it for ten years and believed that he was telling you the truth. I am not sure that you would have had the courage to ask another apostle if he ever sinned and heard him say, "He does little ones and not very often."

Do we take these two apostles that I met at their word? Is is really possible not to be sinning? Do we really take Paul at his word, that the old man can be crucified and we can be a New Creation with Jesus living in us? Does Christ really have the ability to come into us, to possess us, and for us to live our lives just as Jesus would live it if He was on earth? Can we really be Jesus' hands and feet in this world? Was Paul being truthful here?

Is it possible to walk in the Spirit each and every day during every moment?

Galatians 5:16

16 I say then: Walk in the Spirit, and you shall not fulfil the lust of the flesh.

Is this really possible? Can we really walk in the Spirit and deny the lusts of the flesh? Is it possible to be a New Creation who lives in the world but has no portion with the world? Is it possible to walk in such a way that we do not get tossed to and fro by the lusts of the world? John seems to think it is possible:

1 John 2:15-17
(NLT)

15 Do not love this world, nor the things it offers you, for when you love the world, you do not have the love of the Father in you. 16 For the world offers only a craving for physical pleasure, a craving for everything we see, and pride in our achievements and possessions. These are not from the Father, but are from this world. 17 And this world is fading away, along with everything that people crave. But anyone who does what pleases God will live forever.

Personal testimony:

For many years since I met a group called the Jesus Christians that lived by the very commands of Jesus very strictly; I have pondered this verse about not loving the world. For 14 years, I have been coming into obedience to this verse. In the past 3 years, whilst only getting $300 per week in income, I have spent close to $11,000 on producing books and ministry. I have also given about $4000 away to poor people and other ministries at that time. Out of $45,000, at least $15,000 has gone to the Lord and His work.

I do not say this to boast in any way, but when one third of your income is going to things of the Lord, you certainly do not have any lust for the things of this world. I am happy that in the past year, about 9000 of my books have been downloaded free on kindle. Do you know that I would give another $15,000 just to turn a lukewarm Christian into a zealous one like myself?

To be free of the world, to give to the Lord like I do, takes practice and love for the Lord and His will in your life rather than your own pleasures.

I do not know if I will ever recover the money I have spent on my books and websites, but I do know this, even if 1% of the people who read my book, The Parables of Jesus made Simple, read it and apply it in their lives, that would be 80 people on fire. If it was 1.5%, then one hundred people would be on fire for the Lord.

I am just one person, but with my money and time, I put 100 people to flight. To me, that is the 100 fold return that I am looking for! I do not go in for that prosperity preaching, I go for the rewards in Heaven and every person I affect is one more person on fire for the Lord.

Since publishing my book, The Prophetic Supernatural Experience, about the gift of prophecy and the role of a prophet today, I have seen over a thousand people download it. About 700 people have downloaded it for free and 300 have bought it for the cheapest price you can charge for a book on Kindle, 99 cents. Now, if only 1% of the people who bought it, read and applied it and became prophets and powerful because of the start that the book gave to them, then that is 10 people that will be as good as me. I have affected 10 people. Little old me! That is a tenfold return that I am looking at!

Jesus wants all of you, just like he has me, in the area of finances at least.

Will you let Him live through you?

Chapter 19

You are a king and a priest!

Scripture records:

Revelation 1:6

6 And has made us kings and priests to His God and Father, to Him be glory and dominion forever and ever. Amen.

Let me tell you a story. One day, Jesus is going to rule on earth for 1000 years. Some people say that Jesus is not going to reign on earth, but I do not believe they are right. It is my personal belief that when Jesus rules on earth, each country is going to have their own monarchy. They will have a royal family that rules the country for generations and generations. Now, the person that is selected to be king over a particular country will be one very special person. He will be like Abraham to God. He will rule and his son or daughter will rule after him and so it will go for 100 years. A lot of people may say that this idea of mine is not a revelation from God to me, but I personally believe that it is.

Jesus will rule as the One world leader. He will be King over all the kings. When he comes to a country, he will be the head of state over that country while he is there.

I just thought I would throw that out there for you to ponder.

Personally, I do not have confidence to call myself a king. I feel that I am a prince with Jesus as my King, but I guess I do not feel worthy to be a king. I guess I have to meditate this one for a while as this is what the Scriptures says I am. I know I have the authority to decree things and I know that in time, if I learn to decree things and pray right, I will have a whole lot of angels going out to perform the words I am creating.

I am very comfortable being called a priest. I have often thought of doing the civil celebrants course and getting a license to marry people and do funerals. One day, I might just do that so I can serve people like a pastor. I have been called as a prophet and minister quite a lot on Facebook and through my books, I have become confident in myself to be like a priest. I fulfill a pastoral role to many on Facebook and so, I am happy to be known as a priest.

I heard of a pastor who was visiting a person in hospital. As he was walking out, someone who had a relative who was dying asked him if he was a priest and if he could perform the last rights on his loved one. The person was desperate as their relative was fading fast. And this pastor thought of this verse and the one elsewhere that says that we are a royal priesthood and thought, "why not?"

He shared the Gospel with the dying man, led him to Jesus and then said a prayer of blessing over the man. This story made me so happy to hear. This is exactly the sort of thing that I would do too.

We are God's representatives on earth. We are to minister to others for Jesus. We are His servants sent to bring love and blessing to others. We are his chosen people. We can be a priest to a dying person.

With this story, I do not mean to offend any people of the Catholic faith. I am not a person who is big on titles. The first apostles did not go to Bible college to get degrees in theology. They got their authority and power off Jesus and their knowledge from the time they spent with Jesus and the supernatural memories they were given by the Holy Spirit. They were called by Jesus, trained by Jesus, appointed by Jesus and they ministered for Jesus in all matters pertaining to the faith. They were the first priests who served the people, and like them, we can be called by God, trained by the Holy Spirit and minister to people as priests.

I hope that you have enjoyed this book. In my simple knowledge of these attributes that we possess as a follower of Christ and my simple pondering of these, I pray it has been a blessing to you. When this book is published, it will have comments on most chapters from other people. And together, I hope that you were really blessed.

If you were really blessed by this little book, could you do me a favor and bless me back by writing a short, honest review of the book and posting it on Amazon where you purchased it?

You can make me a friend on Facebook or contact mme via email at survivors.sanctuary@gmail.com

You can read more about me or read any of my books for free at http://www.matthewrobertpayneministries.net